PRESENTED TO:

The Deckers

♡ FROM:

Grandma Lil + Grandpa Doug

ON THE OCCASION OF:

♡ U

GRANDMA'S GOSPEL

by SCHARLOTTE RICH · illustrated by JOY ALLEN

WATERBROOK
PRESS

To Stephanie, Sarah, and Steve, with love—S.R.

To Cora, my friend and mentor,

the light that brought the scriptures into my life—J.A.

GRANDMA'S GOSPEL
PUBLISHED BY WATERBROOK PRESS
5446 North Academy Boulevard, Suite 200
Colorado Springs, Colorado 80918
A division of Random House, Inc.

Unless otherwise noted, Scripture quotations are from *The Holy Bible,*
New International Version (NIV) © 1973, 1984 by International Bible Society,
used by permission of Zondervan Publishing House. Scripture quotations
marked (NLT) are taken from the *Holy Bible, New Living Translation,*
copyright © 1996. Used by permission of Tyndale House Publishers, Inc.,
Wheaton, Illinois 60189. All rights reserved. Scripture quotations marked
(TLB) are taken from *The Living Bible,* copyright © 1971. Used by permission
of Tyndale House Publishers, Inc., Wheaton, Illinois 60189. All rights reserved.

ISBN 1-57856-153-1

Library of Congress Cataloging-in-Publication Data
Rich, Scharlotte.
  Grandma's gospel / by Scharlotte Rich; illustrated by Joy Allen.—1st ed.
    p. cm.
  Summary: Presents retellings of several familiar Bible stories along with prayers and
related activities.
  ISBN 1-57856-153-1
    1. Bible stories, English. 2. Christian children—Conduct of life—Juvenile literature.
  3. Christian children—Religious life—Juvenile literature. [1. Bible stories. 2. Christian life.]
  I. Allen, Joy, ill. II. Title.

BS551.2.R46 2000
220.9'505—dc21   99-047799

Printed in the United States of America
2000—First Edition

10 9 8 7 6 5 4 3 2 1

Table of Contents

CHAPTER ONE

The Lunch That Fed Everyone

SHARING

*This story is adapted from
John 6:1-15; Matthew 14:13-21; Mark 6:32-44;
and Luke 9:10-17.*

It was a blue-sky day, a good day to go visiting!

Mom piled Katie and Josh into the car and drove to Grandpa and Grandma's house. On the way the kids argued about anything and everything! Do you ever have days like that at your house?

"I need to run some errands," said Mom when they arrived. "Do you mind watching the kids for a while?"

"Of course not," said Grandma with a hug. "Come in! Come in!"

"Why, Katie!" Grandma said. "What's the matter? Why are you crying?"

Katie pouted. "Josh won't let me play with his soccer ball! He never wants to share with me!"

"She always wants to grab my stuff!" complained Josh. "She doesn't share her things either."

"Hmmm," Grandma said thoughtfully. "You know, this reminds me of a Bible story. Let me find it in my big book and tell it to you." So they all sat around the table eating cookies while Grandma told the story of a boy who learned to share.

Once, a long time ago, there was a little boy. The Bible doesn't tell us his name, so we will call him Eli.

Eli was small, but he had several important jobs to do around his home. He fed the chickens and ran errands. And he always helped his mother whenever she needed him.

His favorite job was to go with his father to the Sea of Galilee. Eli's father was a fisherman. Fishermen work hard. Eli would help him salt and dry the fish whenever there was a big catch.

"You are a good one, my son! When you are old enough to come out in the boat and pull in the nets, we will be a great team!"

Eli laughed as he worked. He looked forward to growing up and being a fisherman just like his father.

Eli was a good helper, but he did not like taking care of his brothers and sisters. They always expected him to share his special things, like the goat-hide ball his father had made. He prized it above everything he owned.

"No, that's mine! Give it to me!" Eli would say.

"Please share your ball with them, Eli," his mother would call. Eli shared while she was watching, but the minute she left, he would grab it back.

Even though they were poor, Eli's family always shared with others. His father helped the neighbors and loaned them his tools. His mother often baked extra bread to give away to anyone who needed it.

"Everything we have comes from God and belongs to Him," his parents said. "God wants us to share our things with others."

Eli wanted to obey his parents, but sometimes it was very hard to share.

On Eli's birthday his parents told him he could spend the day with his friend Caleb.

When they finished their work, Eli and Caleb ran to the lake. They played games with Eli's ball until they were hot, tired, and hungry.

"I'm starving! Let's eat!" Eli shouted. They took the lunch basket his mother had filled with five small loaves of bread and two dried-and-salted fish, and they looked for a shady spot where they could sit down.

As they climbed over a nearby hill, they saw thousands of people. What could be happening?

"Jesus is here!" someone told them excitedly. "He has been healing sick people and making blind people see!"

"He healed my mother!" said a smiling girl.

"He is going to be our king!" a tall man shouted.

"I think He must be the Messiah," whispered another.

Eli and Caleb ran in and out of the crowd until they reached the front, where they plopped down close to Jesus. A funny feeling went through Eli's body as Jesus spoke about loving other people and sharing. He had never heard anyone speak like this! He edged closer and drank in the words like a thirsty child.

When Jesus said that He was the Son of God, Eli knew it was true. Eli prayed and asked God to forgive him for being selfish. He was sorry for the way he had treated his brothers and sisters.

Immediately he felt different. He smiled at Jesus. Jesus smiled back as if He knew Eli's thoughts.

Jesus knew the people were hungry. He told His disciple Philip that the crowd needed food.

Philip panicked. "But it would take more than two hundred denari just to buy a little bit of bread for each person!" he said. In those days it took a whole day of work just to earn one denari. And there were so many people to feed!

Eli heard them speaking and shyly tugged at the robe of one of the disciples. It was Andrew.

"Excuse me, sir," Eli said. "I have some food I want to share. It's not much, but maybe it could feed a few people."

Andrew told Jesus about Eli's lunch. "Have all the people sit down," Jesus said with a smile.

The huge crowd spread out over the hills. There were people as far as Eli could see! Jesus calmly took the five small loaves of bread from Eli and gave thanks to God. Then He began giving out the bread and the fish, as much as everyone wanted.

The people ate and they ate and they ate.

The food Jesus gave never ran out!

Finally, when everyone was full to bursting. Jesus told His disciples to pick up everything that was left over. They gathered up two...four...six... eight...ten...TWELVE baskets of left-over bread from the five small loaves Eli had shared.

Everyone was amazed! Eli's eyes were as big as the baskets! It was a miracle! Jesus had fed thousands of people with *one small lunch.*

"Wow!" whispered wide-eyed Katie.

"What happened after that?" asked Josh.

"The Bible doesn't tell us what happened to Eli," Grandma answered. "But you're never the same after you meet Jesus! I imagine that Eli became a different boy who loved to share everything he had. He learned that God makes even His smallest gifts big enough to share."

"You can have the last cookie, Katie," Joshua said.

"No, you can take it," said Katie with a smile.

"Let's share it!" they laughed together. And Grandma gave them both a big hug!

God loves a cheerful giver.

—2 Corinthians 9:7

Where your treasure is, there your heart will be also.

—Luke 12:34

Some Things to Think About

1. Do you have something you can share?

2. Is it sometimes hard for you to share? Why?

3. How can you share your time with someone?

PRAYER TIME

Dear Jesus,

Thank You for giving me so many good things. Please help me share with other people.

In Your name. Amen.

CHAPTER TWO

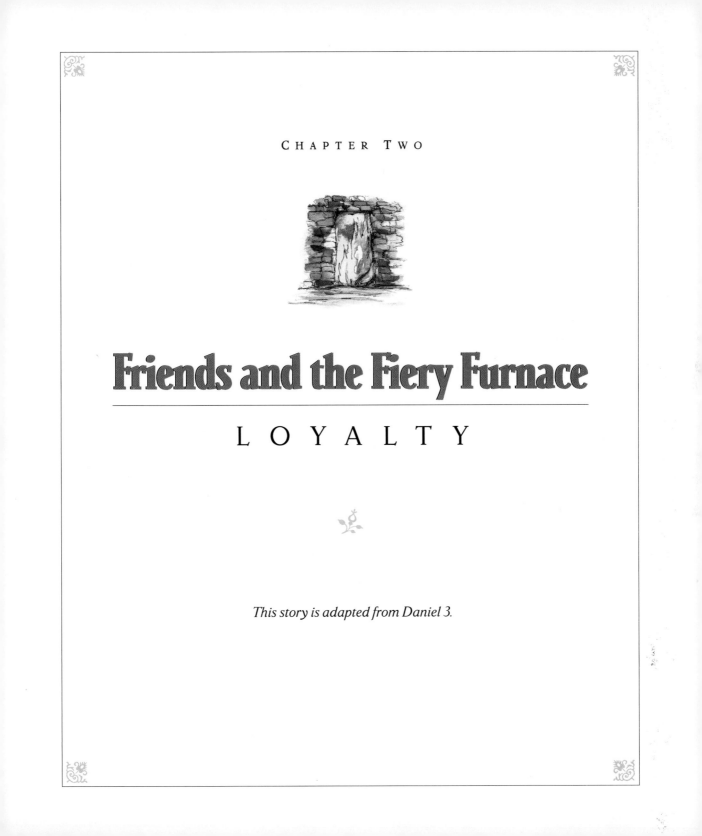

Friends and the Fiery Furnace

L O Y A L T Y

This story is adapted from Daniel 3.

W hat's wrong, Josh?" Dad asked as Josh missed another basket.

Josh sighed. "Brandon is running in the school election, and he wants me to help him. We've been friends a long time, and he's a good guy, but some kids make fun of him. He prays at lunch, has a Bible in his locker, never swears, and sticks up for little kids. I want to help him, but I really want to get along with everybody. I *don't* want to stand out!"

"Good friends who obey God are pretty special," said Dad. "Let me tell you a Bible story that Grandma told me when I was your age."

A long time ago, King Nebuchad-
nezzar had a gigantic golden statue
made. It was ninety feet high and
nine feet wide. He set it up where
everyone could see it. Then he com-
manded all the important people for
miles around to come to a fancy party.

There the king's messenger said,
"Listen, everyone! The king has a new
law. Whenever you hear the king's
musicians play their horns, you must
stop whatever you are doing, bow
down, and worship this idol. Anyone
who disobeys will be thrown into a
hot fiery furnace and burnt to a crisp!"

Then the musicians began to play,
and all the people quickly bowed
down to the statue.

Whoops!

Not everyone bowed!

Three young men decided not to bow down to the statue because they knew that it is wrong to worship anything but God. So when everyone else bowed down, these three friends stood up. It was a very scary thing to do, but they stuck together and encouraged each other to do what was right.

Their names were Shadrach, Meshach, and Abednego. They stood out from the others, and some people didn't like them because they were different.

Those people ran to the king. They whined, "O most wonderful King, some people aren't bowing down to the statue! They aren't worshiping any of your other idols either! Didn't you say that they would be thrown into the furnace? We just wanted to help out and let you know what has been going on!"

But what they really wanted to do was cause trouble for the three friends.

The king was furious! He had the three young men brought to him.

"Is it true that you are not obeying my law?" shouted the king. "I will give you one more chance! Fall down and worship the idol, and I will forgive you! If you don't, you will be thrown into the furnace, where *no* god can rescue you!"

But Shadrach, Meshach, and Abednego stood together and answered the king, "We cannot worship the golden idol. Our God can save us from the fiery furnace. But even if our God decides not to save us, we will not bow down or worship any other god except Him."

Whoa! This made the king even angrier. He ordered the furnace to be made *seven* times hotter than it was before! Then he ordered his soldiers to tie up the three friends and throw them right into the middle of the terrible fire.

When the soldiers obeyed, the heat from the fire was so hot it killed them! Shadrach, Meshach, and Abednego fell into the fiery furnace as it roared with heat.

The king jumped up from where he was watching. "Look! There are four people in the fire, not three. There are four men walking around in the fire, and they are not hurt! The fourth one looks *wonderful*, like a son of the gods!"

The king walked to the front of the furnace in wonder and shouted, "Shadrach! Meshach! Abednego! Come out!"

It was a miracle! Everyone's jaws dropped down to their toes as the three friends walked out of the furnace totally unharmed. Their hair was not singed. Their clothes were not burnt. They didn't even smell like smoke!

The king said, "Praise the God of these three friends who sent His angel to rescue them! They were willing to defy me and die rather than worship other gods. Now I have a new law. No one can say anything against their God, for no other God can save people in this way." And he honored the three friends and gave them good jobs in his kingdom.

"So, you see, Josh," Dad said, "it's good to have true friends who keep you accountable. Friends help each other stand up for what is right. And if you fall, they are there to pick you up."

Josh thought for a moment. "I guess I've always known what I need to do. I was just afraid of being different. But Brandon is a good friend. And there are several other kids who want to help. We just need to stick together and help each other do what is right. If God was in the fiery furnace, I'm sure He's in our school, too."

He who walks with the wise grows wise.

—Proverbs 13:20

Some Things to Think About

1. Read Ecclesiastes 4:9-12. What does this tell you about the importance of family and friends?

2. How can you be a good Christian friend to others?

3. Write down the things you believe in.

4. Ask God to give you a friend who will stand with you. Look for ways you can be loyal to someone else. Encourage each other to follow God.

P R A Y E R   T I M E

Dear God,

Help me to be wise in choosing my friends. Help me to be a good friend who helps others stand strong for what is godly and right.

In Jesus' name. Amen.

CHAPTER THREE

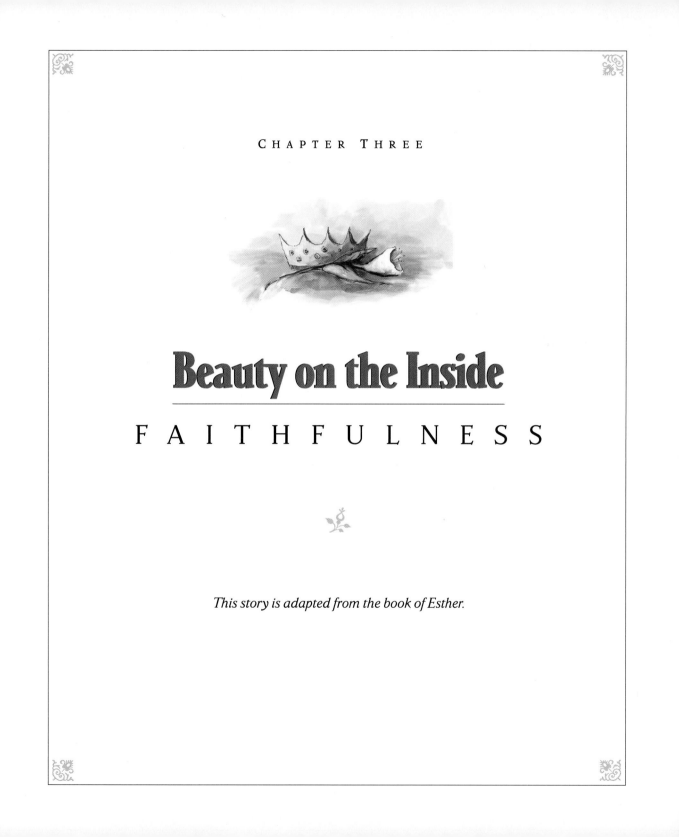

Beauty on the Inside

F A I T H F U L N E S S

This story is adapted from the book of Esther.

"Grandma," said Katie, "will I be pretty when I grow up? I don't look like those girls on TV and in magazines. I want to be taller."

"Katie," smiled Grandma, "God made us all special, each in a different way, just like flowers. Some people are tall, some are short, some have dark hair and dark skin, some have red hair and freckles, or cute brown ponytails. But God made us all like Him, so we all have some beauty somewhere.

"It's more important for you to be beautiful inside than outside. Let me tell you a Bible story about someone whose real beauty was inside."

King Xerxes was a show-off. He thought that
owning lots of beautiful things made him important. He needed to feel important because he didn't
know God loved him. So he invited people to come
and look at all the fancy things he owned. He had
couches of gold and silver in his garden, but the
poor people in his kingdom slept on the ground.

One day the king invited everyone to a banquet that lasted seven days! After showing off everything, drinking too much wine, and acting very important, he ran out of things to say. So he called for his wife, Queen Vashti, to show off her beauty and the jewels he had given her. He sent orders for her to wear her crown. But Queen Vashti refused to come and show off before all the strangers at his party.

This made the king look foolish. He became angry and listened to bad advice from his friends. They urged him to get rid of the queen and find a new one. So King Xerxes sent Queen Vashti away.

The king searched the entire kingdom for a new queen. She had to be very pure and, of course, very pretty.

Near the palace lived a Jewish man named Mordecai. He had an adopted daughter named Esther, who loved God and was very beautiful. The king's messenger ordered her to go to the palace to be judged by the king. She told no one that she was a Jew.

Esther was kind to everyone and made many friends in the palace. When it was time for the king to choose a new queen, he chose Esther. The king was so pleased with Esther that he threw another big party to celebrate their marriage.

Mordecai was worried about Esther and often came to the palace gate to see if she was being treated kindly. One day when he was there, he overheard two men talking about an evil plan to kill the king!

Mordecai ran to tell Esther about the plan. Esther warned the king and saved his life. The king was so pleased with Esther and Mordecai that he had the story written in a special book where all important things of the kingdom were written.

Now, there was an evil man who worked for the king. His name was Haman. Haman thought a lot of himself and was very puffed up with his own importance. He wanted everyone to bow down to him, just as they bowed to the king. But Mordecai the Jew would not bow. He bowed only to God.

Haman complained to the king. "The Jews are always causing trouble!" said Haman. "Please give me your permission to get rid of them!" The king agreed to Haman's plan.

Wicked Haman rubbed his hands and smiled. He wrote a letter and sent it to everyone in the kingdom. The letter said that on a certain day, all the Jews were to be killed.

Every Jew in the land was terribly afraid. When Mordecai read the letter, he wailed and tore his clothes. Then he stopped crying and sent a message to good Queen Esther. "Please go and beg the king to change his mind and let the Jews live!" he wrote.

Now, no one was allowed to see the king without a special invitation, not even his family. Coming into the king's presence without permission meant certain death!

But Mordecai begged Esther to try. "Everyone will die if you don't talk some sense into the king. Maybe God made you queen just so you could save your people from death."

Esther prayed and then said, "All right! I will go and try to save my people. But you must ask all the Jews in our country to pray for God to help me. They must not eat or drink for three days, and they need to pray constantly. My servants and I will pray and fast too. Then I will go and talk to the king, even though I may die."

After three days of praying.
Queen Esther was ready. She put on
her best royal clothes and walked
bravely into the courtyard of the king
because she knew God was with her.
When the king saw her, he smiled.
He was pleased that she had come to
see him.

"What do you want, dear Esther,
my queen?" smiled the king. "I will
give you half of my kingdom!"

"All I desire is to have you come
to a small dinner party I have planned
for Haman," said Esther with great
relief.

Meanwhile Haman was up to his usual dirty tricks. He had a large platform built and planned to ask the king to hang Mordecai on it.

But that night, God intervened and began to answer all the prayers of His people, including Esther. The king could not sleep, so he asked a servant to read the kingdom's special book of events to him. The servant read of the time when Mordecai reported the two men who had planned to kill the king.

"Hey!" said the king. "This man needs to be honored for his good deed."

Haman went to ask the king to hang Mordecai. But before he could ask, the king asked Haman to plan a ceremony for a special person. Haman thought the king meant to honor him, so he thought up a fancy plan for himself.

"Why," Haman said, "give him one of your own royal robes and a special royal horse to ride. Then have your servants parade him around, telling everyone the king is very proud of him."

"Great idea," said the king. "Go immediately and honor Mordecai!"

Haman was shocked, but he obeyed. After honoring Mordecai, Haman hurried to the palace for Esther's banquet with the king.

As they ate, Queen Esther told the king she needed a favor. "There is an enemy who is planning to kill me and all of my relatives and friends. We need your protection!"

The king was furious. "Who would dare to plan this?" he demanded.

"Haman planned it!" answered Esther.

The king became so angry that he rushed out to the garden to think. Haman quickly begged Esther to save his life.

Just then the king returned. He called for his soldiers to arrest Haman. One of the king's servants told him about the platform Haman had built to hang Mordecai.

"Hang Haman from it!" said the king. "That will be perfect justice."

Esther told the king that Mordecai had raised her and cared for her like a father. So the king called for Mordecai and honored him.

Then Esther fell at the king's feet and begged him once again. "My king, please send out an order and cancel the plans to kill the Jews. I could not bear to see all my family and friends killed." By law, the king could not cancel Haman's plans, so instead he sent out a new order that allowed the Jews to defend themselves. On the day the Jews were to be killed, they fought back bravely and lived!

God's people were saved, due to one young woman's bravery and faithfulness and the prayers of many people. There was a great joyful celebration all over the land. Jews still celebrate that day every year on a special Jewish holiday called Purim.

"So," Grandma asked, "who in the story was beautiful on the inside?"

"Well," said Katie, "Esther's courage and faith in God made her beautiful inside. I think the king found her beautiful because he could see the love for God in her face. Haman had beautiful clothes and fancy rings, but he was ugly inside because of the way he treated others. So how do you get beautiful on the inside, Grandma?"

"You keep your eyes on God and reflect His beauty," Grandma said with a smile.

"It's a good thing Jefferson's so beautiful on the inside!" laughed Katie.

Charm is deceptive, and beauty is fleeting;
but a woman who fears the LORD is to be praised.

—Proverbs 31:30

Some Things to Think About

1. List some ways people can be beautiful on the inside.

2. Can you remember a time when someone acted in a beautiful way toward you?

3. Make a plan to spend time in the Bible and in prayer this week. What part of the Bible will you read?

4. Ask God to help you see others' "inside beauty" and not focus on the way they look.

PRAYER TIME

Dear God,

Please help me spend time with You so I can be beautiful on the inside. Please keep my feet on the right path. Help me to obey the things You teach in the Bible.

In Jesus' name. Amen.

Keep Off the Sand!

O B E D I E N C E

This story is adapted from Matthew 6; 7:24-27;
Luke 6:47-49; and Ephesians 6:1-4.

Josh was in really big trouble. He had been told he could not do something. But he went ahead and did it anyway, and then he lied about it. Now he was grounded, big time! His mom had taken Katie to a birthday party and left Josh working at Grandma's house.

"I did a really dumb thing," said Josh as he helped Grandma wash windows. "But I wish there weren't so many rules to obey. Do this. Don't do that. It burns up my brain trying to remember it all."

"Jesus thought obeying rules was pretty important," replied Grandma. "He proved it with His own obedience to God's rules. Let me tell you a story He shared about a wise man and a foolish man."

One day two young men set out on their life journey. Their Master gave them a special Book of specific instructions to help them on their way. He also gave them each a brilliant light to guide them.

The wise man read his Book every day and kept it close to him. "There are a lot of things in here that I need to learn," he marveled.

The foolish man packed his Book on his donkey. "I'll keep it there so it won't get dirty," he said. "I'll take it out and read it when I have more time." But he never read it. One day it fell in the dust, and the man didn't even notice.

When the young men arrived in their new country, there were two roads to choose from. One road was wide and flat. Most of the other travelers were taking that road. They were all laughing and fooling around.

The other road was narrow and went uphill. Only a few people chose that road.

The wise man looked in his Book for directions. "This is the road the Master says to take," he said.

"What?" interrupted the foolish man. "You must be kidding! The wider road is much easier to use, and everyone is taking it! I will not take the road the Master said to take. The Master was wrong!" And so the two men parted.

The wise man traveled along the narrow, difficult road. He stopped to help people along the way, so it took him quite awhile. But the trip was worth it. When he reached the end, he found himself on a high hill that looked out over the ocean. He walked around and found just the place to build his house. The land was sturdy and rock-solid.

"The Master's Book says to build my house on the rock, so I will," he said.

The wise man built a strong house. He searched far and wide to find the best materials and worked hard until dark every day. It would have been easier for him to use some of the broken wood and poor soil he found nearby, but he wanted to build a home where the Master would be comfortable.

"This will be a house to please my Master," he vowed. And whenever he made mistakes, which happened quite often, he stopped, prayed that the Master would forgive him, and went back and made things right.

Finally he stood back and said, "It's not perfect, since I am just an ordinary man. But I have followed the instructions in the Book, and I have prayed that God will bless it with His grace. I am finished."

Then he remembered to do one more thing. He placed the brilliant light the Master had given him on a tall stand, so that everyone passing by, even the ships out on the sea, would be cheered by the light and be able to find their way in the darkness. Then he went about doing his Master's business.

Meanwhile the foolish man was busily building his own house.

"Bother!" he grumbled. "I have lost the Book of instructions the Master gave me. Too bad! I can do just as well by myself."

Then he put down the light the Master had given him and covered it with a bowl to keep it safe.

The foolish man glanced around and found some soft sand.

"Ah," he said confidently, "this place will be easy to build upon."

He found some wood that the sea had washed up and made some bricks from dirty sand. He was a lazy builder. He did whatever was easiest and ended up building a shoddy, sloppy shack.

As he worked he sang, "Why take time to stop and measure? I'd rather play and eat for pleasure." But his house was made for fools. He hadn't followed God's rules. He finished quickly and sat down to eat, drink, and rest. He looked up the hill and laughed at the wise man who was working so hard.

Later that same week a great wind arose, bringing an unnatural darkness to the day. Thunder rolled! Lightning flashed and crackled. The rain came down in torrents.

At the wise man's house, the wind howled fiercely around every corner, but it couldn't get in! The wise man sat quietly reading the Book in his snug warm house as the water began to rise. Boats coming in out of the storm could see the Master's light and were safely guided home. The wise man welcomed anyone needing shelter.

The storm pounded and howled at the little house, but it stood firm because it had been built on a strong foundation.

Crash!

Down below, the foolish man's house was washed away in seconds. His disobedience and laziness had cost him greatly! The Master had told him what to do, but he disobeyed and chose to go his own way.

"God loves you and knows what's best for your life," said Grandma. "He made rules to protect you and help you grow to be wise.

"Your parents have rules for you because they love you. Your school has rules because they want the best for you. Games have rules, and cars in traffic have rules. If there were no rules, the world would be a pretty awful place."

"Yeah, that makes sense," agreed Josh. "I really want to do the right thing."

"Then be obedient," advised Grandma. "Not to impress people watching you, but to please God. Obey even when no one is looking."

"I will," replied Josh. "I want to be a wise person, no matter how hard others tug me to go the wrong way!"

*Do not merely listen to the word, and so deceive yourselves.
Do what it says.*

—James 1:22

Some Things to Think About

1. Do you ever act differently when no one is watching you?

2. Talk about a time when you made some foolish choices. What happened? What might have happened if you had obeyed God's Word instead?

3. Talk about a time when you were obedient to God's Word. What happened? What might have happened if you had disobeyed?

PRAYER TIME

Lord Jesus,

Please help me to be obedient and make good choices. Help me grow up to be wise.

Amen.

CHAPTER FIVE

The Good Neighbor

K I N D N E S S

This story is adapted from Luke 10:25-37.

The whole family was pitching in at the food pantry, packaging food to deliver to the poor.

"It's good to help our neighbors," said Grandpa.

"But this isn't for our neighbors," said Katie. "They just went to the store yesterday!"

"Katie," said Grandma, "Jesus taught the crowds that followed Him the two greatest commandments. Do you know what they are?"

"Isn't the greatest commandment to love God?" interrupted Josh.

"And the second one is to love your neighbor," answered Katie.

"You two are pretty smart cookies!" Grandma exclaimed. "Let me tell you about a lawyer who tested Jesus with questions about neighbors."

"Well, just who is my neighbor that I'm supposed to love?" asked the lawyer.

Jesus, being patient with the man, told him a story:

"There once was a man going on a trip from Jerusalem to Jericho. The road was rocky and cut across the desert. The man had walked for a long way in the hot sun. Suddenly some evil men jumped him, beat him up terribly, and robbed him. They took everything he had, even his clothes and shoes. Thinking he was dead, they ran away, leaving him by the side of the road.

"Not long afterward, a Jewish priest walking down the same road saw the man lying there. But he didn't stop to help. He crossed to the other side of the road. There was a Jewish religious law against touching dead people, so the priest reasoned that the man was already dead and didn't need help. But he didn't check. He just hurried selfishly along on his own way. So the poor man lay there in the hot sun, bleeding into the dust.

"Then a Levite, another very religious man, came down the same road. When he looked at the man lying there, he could not tell if the man was a neighbor or a fellow Jew, so he decided that he did not need to get involved. He walked by even faster on the other side of the road. The poor wounded traveler continued to lie there alone, suffering in great pain.

"Next down the road came a man from Samaria. Now, Jews looked down on Samaritans. In fact, the two groups of people weren't even friendly to each other. This Samaritan was on a journey and still had a long way to go. But when he saw the injured man lying in the dust, he felt compassion for him, even though he was a stranger. He lifted the man up, cleaned and bandaged his wounds, and put him on his own donkey. The injured man rode while the Samaritan walked beside him through the hot desert.

"The Samaritan and his donkey took the man all the way to the next village. There he looked around and found a room at an inn. He cleaned the man up, fed him, and made him rest.

"Then the Samaritan took two silver coins from his pouch and gave them to the innkeeper. 'Take good care of this man,' he said. 'When I return from my trip, I will pay you for anything else he needs.' Then the Samaritan left, not even knowing the name of the man he had helped."

Then Jesus asked the lawyer,
"Which of the three men was a neighbor to the man attacked by robbers?"

"Well, it was the man who helped
him," answered the lawyer.

"Then you go and do the same,"
said Jesus.

"So who is our neighbor?" Grandma asked with a smile.

"Anybody that God puts in front of us who needs help!" answered Katie.

"Yeah," said Josh. "Whenever we have the chance to help someone, that is helping our neighbor."

"And this neighbor needs your help right now!" called Grandpa. "Come use your strong young arms to help me carry these cans to the pantry!"

"Love the Lord your God with all your heart and with all your soul and with all your strength and with all your mind";
and, "Love your neighbor as yourself."

—Luke 10:27

Some Things to Think About

1. Who is your neighbor?

2. How can you be a good neighbor?

3. How can you be a good neighbor to someone who lives in another country?

P R A Y E R   T I M E

Dear Lord,

Please give me a kind heart and help me to see people the way You see them. Show me ways in which I can be a good neighbor this week.

In Jesus' name. Amen.

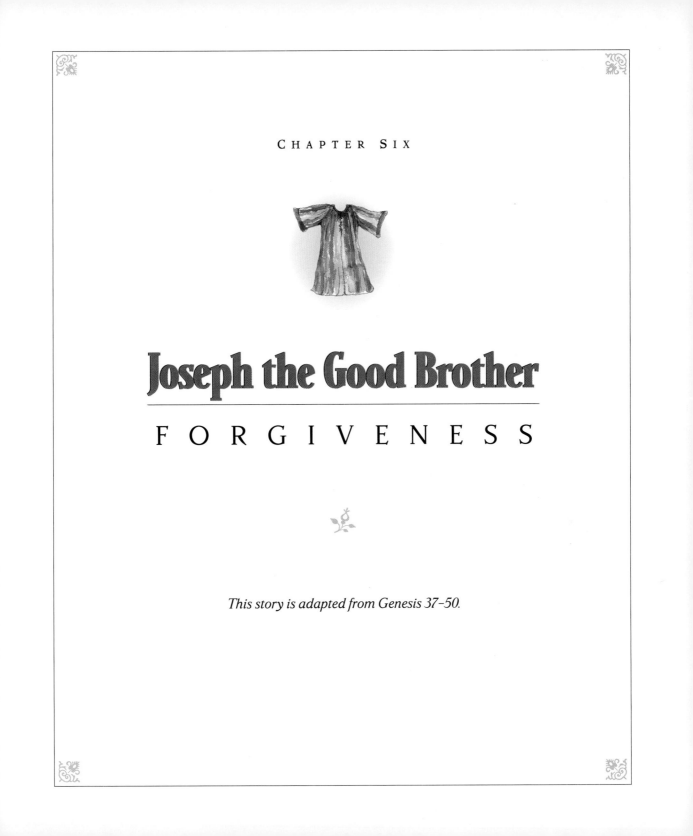

CHAPTER SIX

Joseph the Good Brother

FORGIVENESS

This story is adapted from Genesis 37–50.

Mom and Grandma were working in the garden together when Josh and Katie got off the school bus. Josh slammed his bag onto the ground as hard as he could. "I hate that coach, and I'm quitting the team!" he snarled.

"What's wrong, Josh?" said Grandma. "Hate is a pretty ugly word."

"I don't care!" yelled Josh. "That's how I feel! Coach has favorites who get to play while I sit on the bench! I work harder than anyone! These guys think they are so cool! They make fun of people and laugh at them, and we all get in trouble with Coach. But it's their fault, and I'll never forgive them!"

"There are girls on my soccer team like that," agreed Katie. "I don't like them either!"

"Well, you know, kids," said Mom, "when you don't forgive people and you keep hating them, the person who really gets hurt is you. Your anger makes Satan happy, the people you're angry with don't care, and the hate just eats you up inside. When things don't seem fair, leave it to God. He's in charge of those kids and the coach.

"Come sit in the shade and have a snack with Grandma and me. We'll tell you a story about a boy in the Bible who really had a reason to hate someone."

Joseph was a teenager in Canaan. He and his eleven brothers were shepherds who cared for large flocks of sheep. Joseph, one of the youngest, was his father's favorite.

Joseph's father, Jacob, gave him a beautiful coat. When his brothers saw the coat they were angry and jealous.

Sometime after Jacob gave Joseph the coat, Joseph had two dreams. In the first dream, he and his brothers were tying up bundles of grain. The bundles his brothers tied bowed down to the bundle Joseph had tied. In the second dream, the sun, moon, and eleven stars, which stood for Joseph's parents and brothers, bowed down to Joseph.

When he told this dream to his family, everyone got mad at him. Even Jacob scolded him and said he didn't think the family would ever bow down to Joseph.

One day Joseph was sent into the fields to find his older brothers and to see how they were doing with the great herds of sheep. When he was still far away, the brothers saw Joseph coming.

"There's that dreamer!" they said. "Let's kill him and throw him in a well!"

"Yes!" said another. "We'll tell Father a wild animal ate him!"

But Joseph's oldest brother, Reuben, stopped them. "No, don't kill him. Just throw him in the well." Reuben planned to sneak back and rescue Joseph later.

The brothers grabbed Joseph, ripped off his special coat and threw him in the well. Then they sat down to eat, feeling glad about the awful thing they had done.

Just then some strangers on camels came by. Judah, one of the brothers, said, "Let's pull Joseph out of the well and sell him."

The other brothers agreed. They sold their brother as a slave to strangers for twenty pieces of silver. The strangers took Joseph to Egypt.

The brothers dipped Joseph's coat in goat's blood and took it back to their father. Their father believed their lies that a wild animal had killed Joseph.

When Joseph arrived in Egypt, he was sold to Potiphar, the captain of the guard for Pharaoh the king. But God took care of Joseph. When Potiphar saw that everything Joseph did went well, he put Joseph in charge of his household. Joseph always stayed close to God and obeyed Him.

Then someone who was angry at Joseph lied and said Joseph had done something bad. Potiphar believed the lie and put Joseph in prison for two years. But even in prison, the guards could see that Joseph followed God and God blessed Joseph. So the guards put Joseph in charge of the prison.

Several times other people had strange dreams. They asked Joseph to tell them what the dreams meant. God showed the meanings to Joseph, and everything that Joseph said about the dreams came true!

Pharaoh soon heard about Joseph and sent for him. "I had dreams about seven fat cows, seven skinny cows, and corn. None of my wise men could explain it. Can you?"

Joseph prayed. Then he said, "God is showing you that our land will have seven years of good crops, then seven years of poor crops. You need to get someone to save food during the seven good years. If you don't, your people will starve during the seven bad years."

"You will do it!" said Pharaoh. "It is clear that God is pleased with your obedience. Everyone will bow to you, and you will be in charge of my whole country. I will be the only person more important than you!"

He dressed Joseph in fine clothes and gave him a gold chain and a gold ring right off Pharaoh's finger. Joseph was given a chariot with fast horses. He ruled over Egypt under Pharaoh. The good years came, and Joseph helped the country save their harvest. Then the bad years came, and there was a famine over the entire world. But Egypt had saved enough food to sell to other countries.

Jacob, Joseph's father, sent ten of Joseph's brothers into Egypt to buy corn. Guess who they ran into? They had to bow down to Joseph, because he was in charge of selling the corn!

Joseph recognized his brothers, but they didn't recognize him. He had been a teenager when they sold him as a slave. Now he was a married man dressed like a king.

He remembered how badly they had treated him. Even so, he missed his family greatly. He pretended not to know them and asked them lots of questions. "Tell me about your home," he said. Joseph wanted to find out if his father was still alive.

The brothers were afraid and begin to argue with each other, not knowing that Joseph could understand their language. Reuben, who had stood up for Joseph so long ago, said, "See! I told you not to sin against the boy Joseph! Now we are paying for it." The brothers agreed they were being punished because of the evil way they had treated Joseph.

When Joseph heard them, he turned away so no one would see him crying. Even after all those years, he was still hurt.

Joseph accused the brothers of being spies. He kept one brother and sent the others back to their country with orders to bring back the eleventh brother, young Benjamin, to prove that they were not spies.

After a long trip, Joseph's brothers returned with Benjamin. They were invited to have dinner at the palace with Joseph, but they were afraid of what he would do. They still did not recognize him.

When Joseph saw his youngest brother, he had to rush out of the room. He cried but dried his face and went back to join the others at dinner.

The next morning Joseph accused the brothers of stealing a silver cup. In reality, he had told a servant to place it in Benjamin's bag. "This thief must stay with me as my slave," said Joseph.

"No!" cried the brothers. "Sadness will kill our father if we do not bring our brother back!"

Then Joseph could pretend no longer. "I am Joseph, your brother, the one you sold!" he cried. His cry was so loud and painful that people all over the palace heard it. His brothers were frozen with fear. They were afraid Joseph would have them killed or thrown into prison.

Instead, Joseph opened his arms wide and called them to him. "Don't be afraid!" Joseph told his brothers. "God has always been in control of my life. He used the bad thing you did to put me in charge of Egypt and save many people from starving to death. You meant to hurt me, but God turned it around and used it for good."

God helped Joseph forgive his brothers and filled his heart with love for his family. Everyone had a wonderful time of love and forgiveness together. Then they had a lot of time to talk and catch up.

Joseph sent for his father. Joseph and his wife showed him their children, Jacob's grandchildren. Then Joseph moved his whole family to Egypt and took care of them during the famine.

Joseph was a faithful and a forgiving man. God rewarded him with a rich and full life. He lived to be 110 years old.

"Josh, do you see how good it is to forgive some-one who has hurt you?" asked Mom. "It isn't a sign of weakness but a sign of strength! Forgiving is hard to do, but if you pray, God will give you the strength to forgive. If you don't forgive people, that anger can stay inside you. It will make your heart hard and make you miserable."

"Man, I guess I do need to change my attitude," said Josh. "Will you pray with me?"

"Me, too," piped up Katie. "I'll work on being nicer to those girls."

"It looks like Jefferson is working on his attitude too!" laughed Mom. "Let's pray."

If you forgive men when they sin against you,
your heavenly Father will also forgive you.

—Matthew 6:14

Some Things to Think About

1. Is there someone you need to forgive?

2. Do you need to ask someone to forgive you?

3. Do you need to ask God to change your attitude toward someone or some situation?

PRAYER TIME

Dear Lord God,

Please forgive me for my sins. Please help me forgive others when they sin against me. Please help me talk to people when there is a problem so my anger won't grow inside me. Thank You for sending Jesus to die on the cross for my sins.

In Jesus' name. Amen.

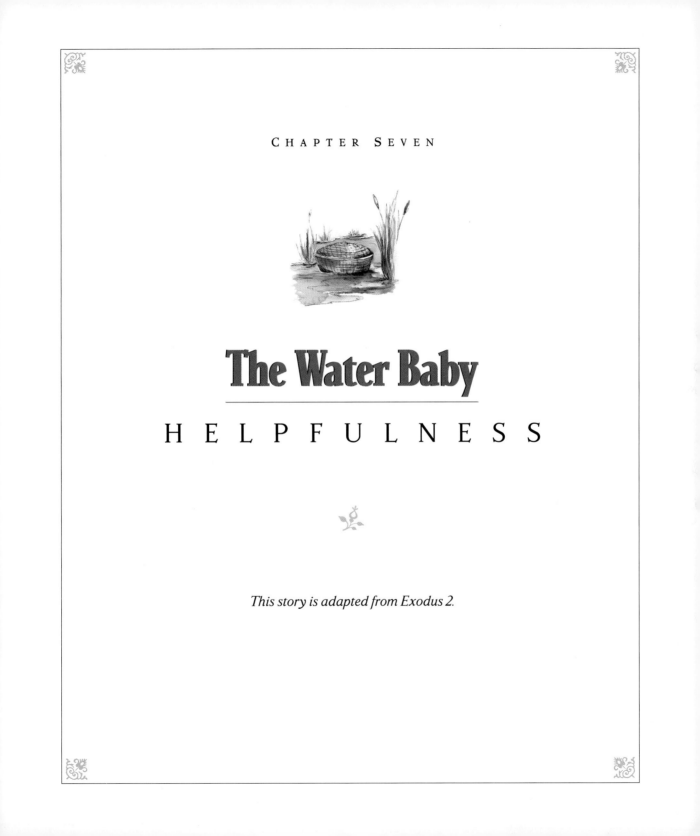

CHAPTER SEVEN

The Water Baby

HELPFULNESS

This story is adapted from Exodus 2.

Josh and Katie's family wanted to give a Christmas present to Jesus. So they decided to help cook and serve a special dinner for homeless people. But Josh had a problem with Katie.

"She's too little," complained Josh. "She'll just get in the way, or she'll break the dishes like she does at home."

"Joshua," said Grandpa, "don't you remember when you were younger? Learning new things isn't always easy."

"Grandma," Katie asked hopefully, "is there a story in your Bible about a little girl who was a big helper?"

"Yes," Grandma said with a smile. "Sit down and I will tell you about a sister who saved her brother's life!"

A very long time ago in Egypt, an evil king called Pharaoh made God's people, the Hebrews, work very hard as slaves.

Pharaoh thought there were too many Hebrews, so he made a terrible law that all Hebrew boy babies were to be thrown into the river and killed.

One brave mother hid her little son at home for three months. But the day came when she couldn't hide him any longer. Then she had an idea.

She made a small basket and covered it with tar so it would float. Then she carefully hid her baby in the basket in the thick, tall grass by the Nile River. But she couldn't stand around and watch him, because Pharaoh's soldiers would find the baby and kill him! What could she do?

The baby had a sister whose name was Miriam. Miriam wanted to help.

"I love my little brother dearly," said Miriam. "I will pretend to work and play down by the river. I will watch over my little brother and not let anything or anybody hurt him."

"I don't know," said her mother. "You are so young, and it is dangerous. What will I do if you get caught? You will have to be very smart and very careful!"

"I will pray, and God will help me," said Miriam. "I am not afraid."

So the sister watched over her little brother as his small basket floated in the river.

Suddenly, her heart jumped and she couldn't breathe!

Pharaoh's daughter was walking down by the river with her servants! She was coming to take a bath. She saw the basket and told her servants to bring it to her.

When she opened the basket, the frightened baby cried. The princess felt sorry for him and said, "Oh, this must be one of the Hebrew babies. He is wonderful! I shall keep him!"

Miriam was afraid, but she thought quickly! She bravely ran up to Pharaoh's daughter and smiled. "May I please help?" she asked. "I could find a woman to take care of the baby for you!"

"Yes, that would be good!" said the princess. So Miriam ran and brought back her own mother, the baby's real mother!

Now the mother was able to safely care for her baby at home until he grew older. But then she had to take him to the palace to live with the princess. That must have been very hard for her and Miriam.

Pharaoh's daughter named the boy Moses, which means, "he came out of the water." Young Moses lived in the palace and was treated as her royal son. He grew up to become a great leader of God's people.

"We don't know much more about Miriam's childhood," Grandma said. "But we do know that she was brave and smart and loved her family. She prayed to God and saved her brother's life."

"Wow," said Josh and Katie together.

Josh ruffled Katie's hair. "I'm sorry I picked on you, Sis! You'll be a big help at the dinner."

Don't let anyone look down on you because you are young,
but set an example for the believers in speech, in life, in love, in faith and in purity.

—1 Timothy 4:12

Some Things to Think About

1. Is there someone younger than you whom you can help? How?

2. Is there someone older than you whom you can help? How?

3. How can older kids be a good example to younger ones?

4. How can you help around your home?

PRAYER TIME

Dear Father God,

Thank You for giving me life so I can serve You by helping other people. Please show me ways that I can please You even though I am young. Help me be a good example to others by the things I say and do.

In Jesus' name. Amen.

Fire from Heaven

C O U R A G E

This story is adapted from 1 Kings 17-18.

Katie and Josh were spending the night at Grandma's house.

Katie called out for Grandma soon after the lights were out. "Grandma, I can't sleep! There are scary things in the dark that will get me! I'm afraid."

Just then Josh padded into the room. "I can't sleep either. I keep thinking about school. Some of the boys were calling me names because I had my Bible with me. They made fun of Jesus and were swearing.

"Sometimes I feel like I don't fit in. I feel alone because I'm a Christian. Did anyone in the Bible ever feel that way?"

"Come and read to us, Grandma. Please?" Katie sniffled. "And can Jefferson curl up on my bed while you read? Just this once?"

"Well, all right. Just this once!" Grandma said with a smile. But she suspected that once the lights were out Jefferson slept anywhere he pleased.

"Now let's see. How about the story of a man who was alone and afraid and how God took care of him?"

"Yeah!" said Josh and Katie. So Grandma sat down and opened her Bible.

A long time ago, after King David and his son King Solomon died, the land of Israel was ruled by very wicked kings. King Ahab was the worst of them. Everyone was afraid of him!

Ahab and his queen, Jezebel, worshiped a false god named Baal and built a large temple for him. They believed Baal had power to bring the sun and rain that made their crops grow. Their army began killing anyone who would not bow to the statues of Baal.

But a man named Elijah was faithful to God and would not bow to Baal. Elijah was a prophet, a person God used to tell people very important things.

God sent Elijah to tell King Ahab and Queen Jezebel that God was angry because they worshiped idols. Elijah pleaded with them to change their wicked ways and worship the one true God instead.

But King Ahab didn't listen to Elijah. He just laughed and made more statues.

Again God warned Ahab through Elijah. Elijah said, "If you don't stop worshiping Baal, there will be no rain in your country for three years."

That would be awful! There would be no water to drink and no way to wash anything. Imagine eating out of the same dirty dishes every day! Yuck!

There would be no rain to grow food. The people and the animals would starve!

But King Ahab laughed an evil little snort. "Hah! I don't believe your God is real. Get out of here! I don't have time to waste listening to you!"

Ahab sent his army to kill Elijah. Elijah was afraid and hid alone in the country. But God protected Elijah. He sent ravens to bring him food. Elijah drank water from a small, cool brook.

Soon the hot sun beat down on the earth. The rivers and lakes began to dry up. All the people were hungry because God had held back the rain and no food could grow. Even Elijah's brook dried up.

After three years, God told Elijah to go speak to the king again. Elijah obeyed even though he was afraid Ahab would kill him. He knew God would go with him.

King Ahab was angry because no rain had fallen. His horses were dying and couldn't pull his chariot.

"King Ahab, it is your own fault that your people are hungry," said Elijah. "You are stubborn. You do not obey God. You have been a bad king to lead your people in worshiping idols."

Ahab became even angrier. But Elijah said, "Meet me at Mount Carmel. We will have a contest to see whose God is real and whose god is phony—your god Baal or the Lord God of Israel!"

When they met at the mountain, thousands of people came to watch.

On one side stood Elijah, all alone because he followed the Lord. On the other side were 450 followers of the idol Baal.

"Okay," said Elijah. "Let's build two big altars out of stone and wood. Put meat on top of them to burn as an offering. You pray to Baal, and I will pray to the Lord. The God who answers by fire is the only true God."

What a crazy morning it was! The prophets of Baal prayed to their idol, but nothing happened. They began jumping around the altar, praying louder. Still nothing happened.

Elijah made a joke. "Hey, you guys! Speak louder. Maybe Baal is busy or on a trip! Maybe he's asleep. You'll have to yell to wake him up!"

The followers of Baal cut themselves with swords to get Baal's attention. The noise and jumping and praying and cutting went on until midnight. But of course there was no answer, because there are no other gods except the Lord.

When Baal's people gave up, Elijah put wood and meat on God's altar. Then he did something weird.

Elijah had people pour jars of their precious water over everything! They did this three times until everything was dripping wet! Then Elijah dug a deep ditch around the altar and filled that with water too.

"How can you burn something that's all wet?" the people wondered.

But Elijah just smiled and prayed, "O Lord God, please answer my prayers so that these people will know you are the one true God and will follow you."

Whoosh! All of a sudden, hot burning fire fell from the sky!

God's fire burned the meat! God's fire burned the wood! God's fire burned the altar stones, the dust, and all the water in the ditch!

The people were astonished and amazed. They fell on their faces in the dust and worshiped God! Then they stood up and shouted with joy. "The Lord! He is our God!"

Elijah ordered the people to kill the evil prophets of Baal so they could not lead anyone in evil ways again.

Then a strong wind blew. The sky became black, and a heavy rain began to beat down on the thirsty land as God blessed His people once again.

"Elijah was afraid," said Grandma, "but God was with him.

"Josh, sometimes you'll have to stand up for what is right. But you won't be alone, because God will stand with you. Katie, you can be brave if you pray and trust God. He will be with you even on the darkest night. Grownups can help too. Don't be afraid to tell an adult when something is bothering you.

"Now let's say a prayer and go to sleep," Grandma said with a yawn.

"Jefferson is already asleep!" laughed Katie.

"Thanks, Grandma," said a smiling Josh. Then he prayed for everyone, even the boys who had made fun of him.

Give all your worries and cares to God, for he cares about what happens to you.
—1 Peter 5:7 (NLT)

Some Things to Think About

1. What are you afraid of? Talk about it with someone who cares about you.

2. Pray about something you are afraid of. Ask God for help.

PRAYER TIME

Dear God,

Please help me to be brave when I am afraid. Please keep me safe. Thank You for watching over me and my family.

In Jesus' name. Amen.

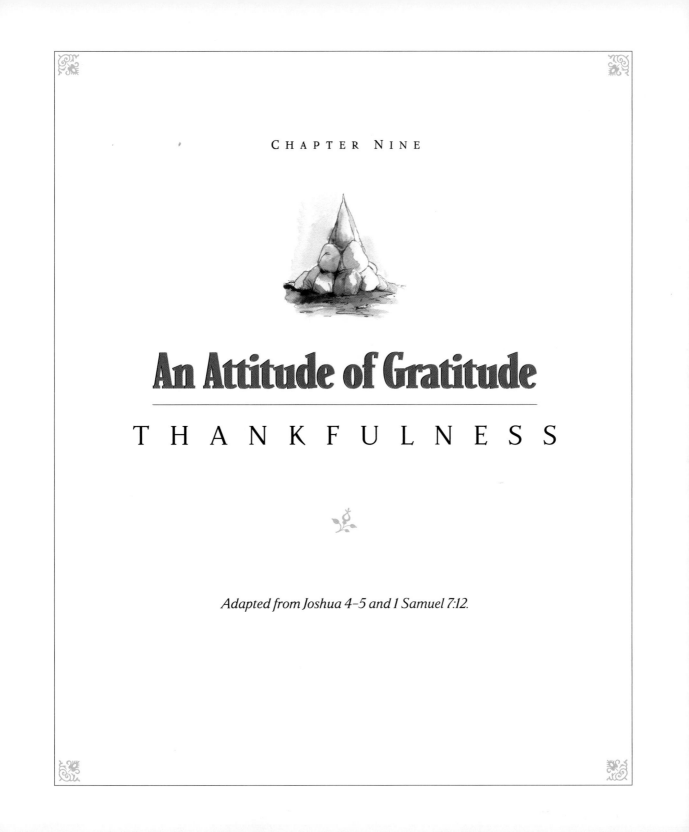

CHAPTER NINE

An Attitude of Gratitude

T H A N K F U L N E S S

Adapted from Joshua 4–5 and 1 Samuel 7:12.

The summer sky was bright and clear at the lake, a perfect spot for the family reunion! Josh and Katie were having fun swimming and canoeing with their cousins.

"This is great!" laughed Katie. "I wish we could stay here all summer."

"Yeah, this is a cool place," agreed Josh, examining a squirming turtle he and his cousin had just caught.

"I see you're counting your blessings," smiled Grandma, returning from a hike. "We have so many! We need to remember blessings like this. Do you know how people in the Bible remembered God's blessings? They didn't have computers or sticky notes, and many of them couldn't read or write.

"There was no television, no newspapers or magazines, and no pencils or paper for ordinary people," said Grandma, taking off her shoes and wading into the cool water. "Storytellers memorized stories and passed on important things that happened in people's lives.

"But there was one very special way for people to remember their blessings. They used memory stones. Let me tell you about those stones."

Joshua was a brave soldier. He led thousands of Israelites across the wilderness to a new home. During their long journey they came to the Jordan River. It was the harvest season, and the water was too high for them to go across the raging river safely.

Joshua prayed to God for help. God told Joshua that He would perform a miracle so that all the people could cross the river. Joshua had the people choose twelve leaders, one from each Israelite tribe. They and the priests would go into the wild river in the morning.

Early the next morning Joshua sent the twelve leaders and the priests, who carried the Ark of God, down to the swirling river. As their toes touched the water, way up the river the water suddenly stopped flowing as though held back by a dam.

The priests stood in the middle of the river holding the Ark of God as the people hurriedly passed across to the other side. All the people were amazed and praised God as they walked across the dry and stony riverbed.

Then Joshua told each of the leaders to take a large stone from the middle of the riverbed. That night they put the stones in a pile and made a special monument where the people camped.

"We will use these stones to help us remember God's blessing in getting us across the river," Joshua said. "Later on, whenever your children see the stones and ask about them, you must tell them, 'They are to remind us of God's amazing miracle, when He stopped the waters of the Jordan River so we could cross.'"

Then Joshua built another monument of stones right in the middle of the dry riverbed. Just as he finished and came out of the river, the water poured into the riverbed again and overflowed the riverbanks!

Many years later, another godly man named Samuel was in a fierce battle with the Philistines. They were the same people who used Goliath the giant to fight against young David. Do you think that David kept the stone he used to kill Goliath as a reminder of God's blessings?

Anyway, the powerful Philistine army was fierce and well-armed with fast chariots, iron swords, and spears. They were coming to attack the frightened Israelites, who were much weaker.

Samuel was giving an offering to God when the Philistines attacked. During the fierce battle, God called out in a mighty voice like thunder. This scared and confused the Philistine army so badly that the Israelites easily beat them. The Israelites were courageous, knowing that God was with them and was blessing them. They chased the Philistine army across two villages. The Philistines were so scared of the Lord that they didn't bother the Israelites for the rest of Samuel's life!

After winning the battle, Samuel built a large stone monument called Ebenezer, which means "stone of help." Every time the people saw it they were reminded to count their blessings. God had saved them! The monument helped them not to worry about the future, because whenever things got tough, they were reminded that God had helped them in the past.

When Grandma finished the story, Josh and Katie and their cousins got together and planned something special. Everyone in the family took turns putting rocks on a pile beside the lake. As they tossed in their stones, they each shared a blessing that God had given them that year.

"I'm thankful for my family," said Katie.

"I'm thankful for the missions trip I went on," Josh added.

Creating a pile of memory stones became a tradition. Every year at the family reunion, the pile of stones grew larger as the families practiced being thankful and, as Josh said, "having an attitude of gratitude."

It is good to say thank you to the Lord, to sing praises to the God who is above all gods. Every morning tell him, "Thank you for your kindness," and every evening rejoice in all his faithfulness.... You have done so much for me, O Lord. No wonder I am glad! I sing for joy.

—Psalm 92:1-2,4 (TLB)

Rejoice in the Lord always. I will say it again: Rejoice!

—Philippians 4:4

Some Things to Think About

1. Try thanking God for something every morning before you get out of bed.

2. See how long a list you can make of things you are thankful for.

3. As a family, keep a list for a year of things you are thankful for. Keep them in a journal or a box. Read them on Christmas Eve or your birthday.

PRAYER TIME

Dear Lord,

Thank You for giving me so many blessings. Thank You especially for _____ (name several blessings).

In Jesus' name. Amen.

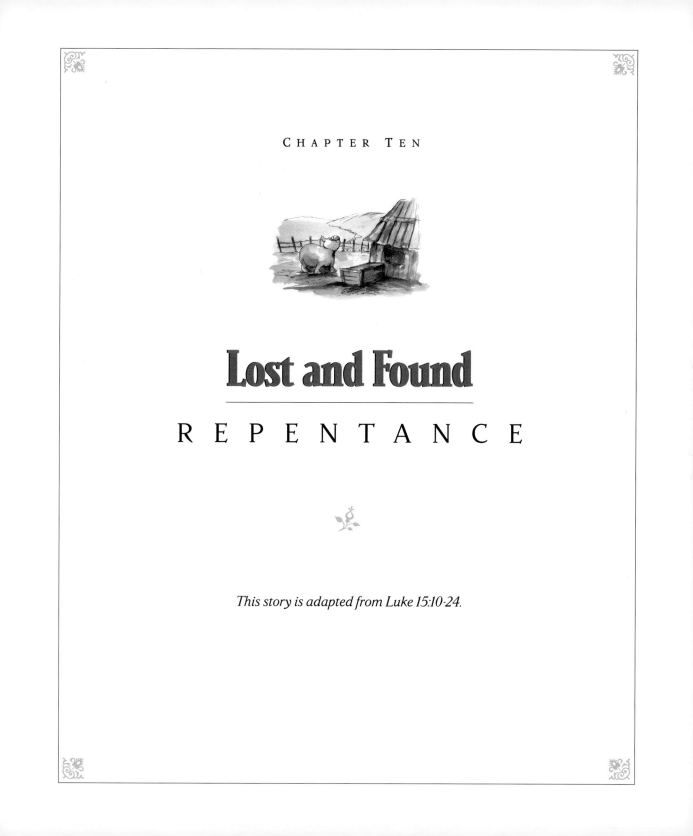

CHAPTER TEN

Lost and Found

R E P E N T A N C E

This story is adapted from Luke 15:10-24.

Later that week, the family sat together around a crackling campfire. They had marshmallows and were making sticky desserts.

Katie and her cousin had gotten into big trouble earlier by disobeying. They were feeling very sorry.

"How do you get to heaven?" asked Katie. "It seems so far away. How does God know what's going on here if He's way up there? And how can He care about me when I do so many bad things?"

"That's a pretty long list of questions," laughed Mom, hugging Katie.

"How about a little bit of Grandma's Gospel?" said Dad with a twinkle in his eye. "Got a good Bible story that will cover all of those questions?"

"Well," said Grandma as she thought a minute, "Jesus answered questions all the time."

Jesus once told a story of a family with two sons. The youngest son thought life at home was boring. He was tired of obeying his mother and father. He wanted to make all his own decisions and run his own life.

So he asked his father to divide up the family property and give him his share of the money from it. Then the young man took the money, packed up all his belongings, and left home for a faraway country.

When he arrived in the new country, everything seemed exciting! He didn't have any rules to obey! He bought food and drinks for strangers and threw big parties for people he didn't know. He spent the money his father had given him without stopping to think what would happen when the money ran out.

One day he found that he had wasted every dollar, every dime, every penny that his father had given him. He turned to his new friends for help, but when they found out his money was gone, suddenly they were gone too! The young man was all alone and penniless.

Then a famine came to the country, and there was very little to eat. The young man talked a farmer into giving him a job feeding and taking care of the farmer's pigs. The pigs were mean, selfish, dirty, and smelly. The young man didn't even make enough money to buy food. He slept with the pigs. After a while he became so hungry that even the pig's food began to look good to him.

As he took care of the pigs, he began to see that they acted just like him and his friends. Each pig wanted his own way. No one would share anything, and they only wanted to please themselves. It was chaos!

The young man began to think of his true home. Even the servants there had plenty of good food to eat. His father loved him. The young man knew that he had been selfish, greedy, and unkind. He was so ashamed.

But he made up his mind. He would return home and beg his father to forgive him. Then he would ask his father if he could work there as a servant. He did not feel worthy to be part of the family since he had acted so selfishly.

So the young man left the pigs and began to walk home. He was hungry and dirty and tired and miserable. He felt that no one could ever love him.

After several long, hard days of walking, at last he set his blistered and bleeding feet on his father's land. He was in dirty rags, and he smelled like the pigs he had been sleeping with.

While the young man was still a long way off, his father looked out over the fields—just as he had every day since his boy left home—searching for a sign of the son he loved so much. The father was filled with joy at the sight of his ragged and dirty son. He ran to him, hugging and kissing him. His son dropped to his knees, saying, "Father, I have sinned against heaven and you. I am not worthy of being called your son!"

But his father called the servants. "Quickly! Bring the best clothes and shoes! Bring a special ring for his finger so that everyone will know he is my son! We will have a wonderful celebration, because my son was dead and now he is alive! He was lost and now is found!"

Then Jesus explained the story. He told His disciples that there is great joy and celebration in heaven when one sinner turns from sin and asks forgiveness.

Grandma smiled and said, "Jesus told us stories of what God is like so people could understand how much God loves us. God is a loving father who waits for us to ask for forgiveness for the wrong things we have done. God loves every person on earth, but sin separates us from His love. Jesus became a bridge across that separation when He died on the cross. Jesus died once for the sins of everyone so He could bring us safely home to God."

Katie and her cousin prayed at the campfire. "Please, God, forgive my sins. Come into my heart and take over my life."

"Now God isn't far away," said Katie, her eyes sparkling. "He's right here in our hearts!"

And don't you know that the angels in heaven danced with great joy that night!

There is rejoicing in the presence of the angels of God
over one sinner who repents.

—Luke 15:10

Some Things to Think About

1. Have you asked God to forgive your sins?

2. Do you have any friends who need to know that God loves them? How can you tell them?

PRAYER TIME

Dear Lord God,

Please forgive me for the things I have done wrong. Please be in charge of my life and help me do what is right. Please watch over my family and me. Please help me share Your love with people who don't know You. Thank You, Jesus, for dying on the cross for me.

Amen.